QUITE MAD

AND OTHER WORKS
BY MOLLY BARKER

The Crossing Press
Freedom, CA 95019

Cover art by Molly Barker
Book design by Molly Barker and Sheryl Karas
Printed in the U.S.A.

Library of Congress Cataloging-in-Publication Data

Barker, Molly.
    Quite mad and other works / by Molly Barker.
        p.   cm.
                . — ISBN 0-89594-700-5 (pbk.)
    1. Women—Humor. 2. Women—Caricatures and cartoons. 3. Mental
illness—Humor. 4. Mental illness—Caricatures and cartoons.
I. Title.
PN6132.W6B37   1994   94-21520
813'.54—dc20   CIP

For Lynda

OUTSIDE THE DOOR

IS A SOUND

LIKE ANIMALS LICKING THEIR LIPS

I CAN'T SLEEP

IT GOES ON AND ON

IF THIS IS A MONSTER

I'M THINKING

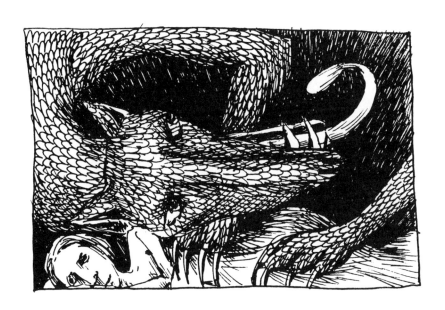

IT'S THE MOST PATIENT MONSTER
I'VE EVER EXPERIENCED

I COULD EITHER LIE HERE

OR GET UP.

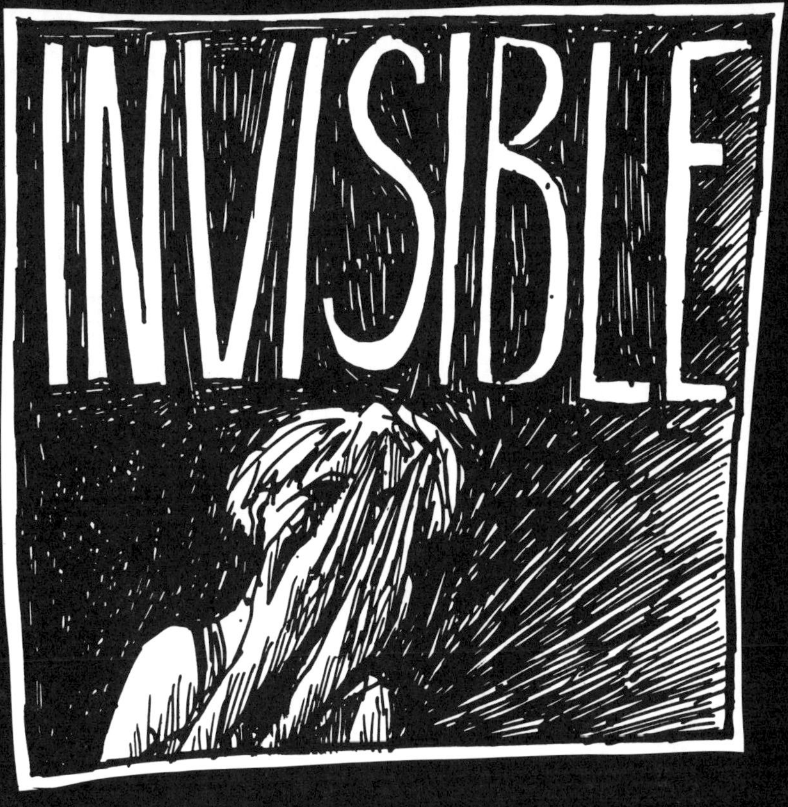
INVISIBLE

IN THE RESTROOM

I REARRANGED MY FACE

BUT LOST IT AGAIN IN THE STALL.

SOMEONE CAME IN

VOMITED EFFICIENTLY FASTER THAN
I COULD PEE

AND RINSED HER HANDS.

SHE TURNED OUT THE LIGHT WHEN SHE LEFT.

I WAS STILL THERE.

SOMETIMES YOU SEE PEOPLE CRAWL

YOU CAN'T BELIEVE SOMEONE COULD GET
SO LOW.

THEN YOU LOOK AT ALL THE OTHERS.
THAT'S WHAT MAKES YOU SICK.

BECAUSE OF COURSE IT'S ALL THE PEOPLE
WHO ALREADY THOUGHT THEY WERE GOD'S GIFT.

NOW THEY FEEL TEN FEET TALLER BECAUSE
OF STANDING NEXT TO A CATERPILLAR.

AND YOU WANT TO SHAKE THEM ALL

INCLUDING THE ONE THAT'S BELLY DOWN
ON THE FLOOR.

BURIED VEINS

THEY'RE ALL OVER THE PLACE!

THE TERRIBLE SINGING NEIGHBOR

THE BEAMING DOWSER

WALL-EYED BABIES

THAT INSIPID TOMCAT

THE PICTURE OF THE QUEEN!

IT'S ENOUGH TO DRIVE A PERSON
TO ANCIENT SECTS

WITH UNDERGROUND CHAMBERS

SCRATCHED SYMBOLS

MAYBE BLOOD

OR AT LEAST TO RIDE THE COLD RAILS

IN SEARCH

AFTERWARDS I JUST WENT

OUT INTO THE FIELD AND CRIED.

I DIDN'T CARE WHO SAW.

IN FACT I WISHED THEY WOULD SEE —

THERE'S NOT ENOUGH OF THAT.

I UNDERSTAND WHY PEOPLE DISCARD
DIRTY BANDAGES IN STERILE OFFICES.

ONCE I LEFT BLOOD FROM PAPERCUTS
ON PAGES I WAS COLLATING IN AN
ASSEMBLY LINE

JUST TO SHOW.

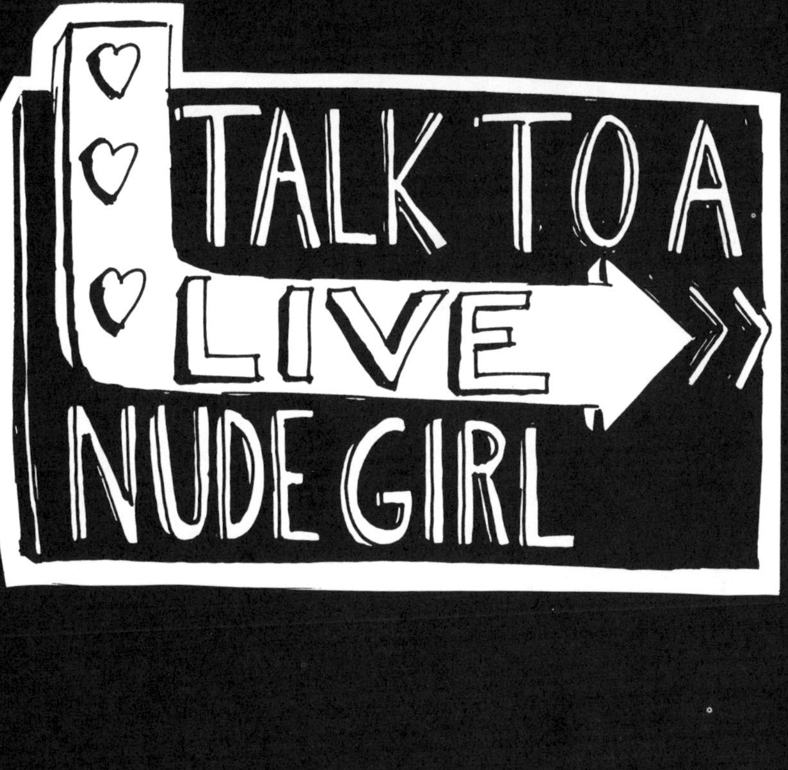
TALK TO A
LIVE
NUDE GIRL

ONE DAY

ALL THE SWEATING

BREATHING

TWENTY-FIVE CENT

NAKED

GIRLS

GIRLS

GIRLS

MIGHT TALK BACK

WHILE THEY HAVE YOU ON THE LINE

AND TELL YOU WHAT THEY REALLY DREAM.

LAID IT IN

LIKE IT WAS DEAD

SPIDER LEGS WAVING

HEAPED THE EARTH ON

HEAVY

PAT IT DOWN

WHAT SPIDER?

DEEP

BELLY
RUMBLE

HEARD THAT DEEP BELLY RUMBLE AND THOUGHT
SURE A BIG TRUCK WAS COMING AND I WAS FLAT.

BUT NEXT I KNEW IT COULDN'T BE AND
THE FIELD WAS SOLID WATER AND THE
CHIMNEYS DOING A JIG.

I JUST WATCHED THIS TREE BENDING OVER.
TREES BEND.

NIGHT AT MY HOUSE WAS DARK. TAKING A
PISS OUTSIDE WAS DARKER. ON THE INSIDE
WE HAD A CANDLE AND THE RADIO ON.
FEEDING US DEATH AND DON'T PANIC BUT
THESE BRIDGES COLLAPSED

AND THEY'RE PRYING PEOPLE OUT OF
CARS AND THE EPICENTER'S IN YOUR
BACKYARD. WELL, WE CLEANED UP
THE KITCHEN PARTLY

AND ATE A SANDWICH IN THE HALLWAY
THAT WAS SAFER FOR THE AFTERSHOCKS.
WONDERING ABOUT PEOPLE.
BECAUSE WE HEARD SOME DIED.

GREY LIGHT IN THE MORNING. ALL THE
CLOCKS STOPPED AND WE JUST WALKED.
SEE WHAT HAPPENED. NO NEWSPAPERS,
NOTHING. IT WAS ALL UP TO US.

THINGS WERE DIFFERENT THAN I'D EVER
SEEN THEM. SAGGING AND NO ONE THERE.
DENNY'S CLOSED. SIDEWALK BROKEN AND
WINDOWS. GLASS EVERYWHERE AND SOME
BUILDINGS DOWN I GUESS.

BUT NOTHING WAS TOO BIG. IT WASN'T
TOTAL CHAOS. PEOPLE RIDING BIKES. IT
WOULD BE BAD IF YOU WERE OUT OF A JOB
OR YOUR HOUSE FELL IN. BUT IT WASN'T
LIKE EVERYTHING CRASHED. TOWN WAS
STILL THERE.

THE THING IS THAT AFTERNOON THE
PAPERS CAME OUT AND WE FOUND OUT
WE WERE DEMOLISHED AND IT WAS A
BIG DISASTER EVERYONE HEARD ABOUT.

PHONES WERE RINGING FROM FAR AWAY
AND THEY'D LEARNED ALL ABOUT THAT
BOY THAT WAS TRAPPED AND EVERYTHING.
IT MADE ME FEEL KIND OF LEFT OUT.

WE DIDN'T EVEN HAVE TV YET AND
EVERYONE ELSE HAD 'HEARD ALL THE
STORIES.

ELLIE SPLIT AFTER THE QUAKE.

THE RADIO WAS REPEATING ITSELF.

THEY GAVE HER FIFTEEN MINUTES IN HER
BUILDING. IT WAS ON ITS KNEES.

THE HARDHAT ESCORT WAITED IN THE HALL
WHILE ELLIE FED HER FISH AND DUG
UP HER YELLOW RAINCOAT

HALF THE BUILDINGS ON HER BLOCK WERE
RED-TAGGED FOR DEMOLITION.

MR. AMALTHUSA WAS IN TEARS.

THE LIQUOR STORE WHERE ELLIE WORKED
HAD BLIND PLYWOOD WINDOWS AND A YELLOW
RIBBON TO KEEP YOU OUT.

ELLIE WASN'T GOING TO WAIT FOR THE
WRECKING BALL.

NEXT MORNING SHE SPIED A MAKESHIFT DEPOT
IN WINCHELL'S PARKING LOT.

BY NOON THE GREYHOUND WAS RUNNING

AND ELLIE WAS ON IT.

VICTORIAN MADWOMEN LIVE IN THEIR NIGHTGOWNS

THEY CAN'T STOP SHRIEKING SO SOMEONE
LOCKED THEM UP.

THEY HANG THEIR HEADS OUT WINDOWS

MAKING A SPECTACLE.

EVERYONE LOVES TO SEE THEM.
THEY'RE QUITE MAD.

IT'S NO LIFE.
DIRTY SHEETS AND TOO MUCH TIME.

HALLWAYS ECHO AND LOCKS CLANG SHUT.
THE WOMEN WHISPER AND CRY.

BUT SOMETIMES IN THE CORRIDORS

SECRETLY THEY SMILE.